Scott Joplin
1868–1917

6 Ragtimes
The Entertainer · Elite Syncopations
Original Rags · Pine Apple Rag
The Cascades · Maple Leaf Rag

With the "School of Ragtime" by /
Mit der „Ragtime-Schule" von /
Avec la «Méthode du Ragtime» par
Scott Joplin

ED 9014
ISMN M-001-11599-5

SCHOTT

Mainz · London · Madrid · New York · Paris · Tokyo · Toronto
© 1997 Schott Musik International GmbH & Co. KG, Mainz · Printed in Germany

6-80

Contents / Inhalt / Contenu

School of Ragtime

by Scott Joplin

Remarks

What is scurrilously called *Ragtime* is an invention that is here to stay. That is now conceded by call classes of musicians. That all publications masquerading under the name of ragtime are not the genuine article will be better known when these exercices are studied. That real ragtime of the higher class is rather difficult to play is a painful truth which most pianists have discovered. Syncopations are no indication of light or trashy music, and to shy bricks at 'hateful ragtime' no longer passes for musical culture. To assists amateur players in giving the 'Joplin Rags' that weird and intoxicating effect intended by the composer is the object of this work.

Exercise No. 1

It is evident that, by giving each note its proper time and by scrupulously observing the ties, you will get the effect. So many are careless in these respects that we will specify each feature. In this number, strike the first note and hold it through the time belonging to the second note. The upper staff is not syncopated, and is not to be played. The perpendicular dotted lines running from the syncopated note below to the two notes above will show exactly its duration. Play slowly until you catch the swing, and never play ragtime fast at any time:

Exercise No. 2

This style is rather more difficult, especially for those who are careless with the left hand, and are prone to vamp. The first note should be given the full length of three sixteenths, and no more. The second note is struck in its proper place and the third note is not struck but is joined with the second as though they were one note. This treatment is continued to the end of the exercise:

Exercise No. 3

This style is very effective when neatly played. If you have observed the object of the dotted lines they will lead you to a proper rendering of this number and you will find it interesting:

Exercise No. 4

The fourth and fifth notes here form one tone, and also in the middle of the second measure and so to the end. You will observe that it is a syncopation only when the tied notes are on the same degree of the staff. Slurs indicate a legato movement:

Exercise No. 5

The first ragtime effect here is the second note, right hand, but, instead of a tie, it is an eighth note: rather than two sixteenths with tie. In the last part of this measure, the tie is used because the tone is carried across the bar. This is a pretty style and not as difficult as it seems on first trial:

Exercise No. 6

The instructions given, together with the dotted lines, will enable you to interpret this variety which has very pleasing effects. We wish to say here, that the 'Joplin ragtime' is destroyed by careless or imperfect rendering, and very often good players lose the effect entirely, by playing too fast. They are harmonized with the supposition that each note will be played as it is written, as it takes this and also the proper time divisons to complete the sense intended:

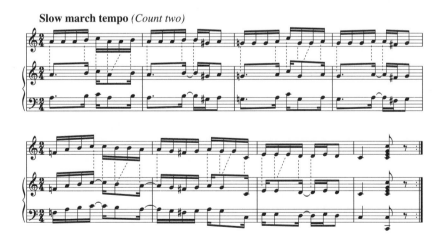

Ragtime-Schule

von Scott Joplin

Vorbemerkung

Was man so gemeinhin, manchmal etwas abwertend, als *Ragtime* bezeichnet, ist ein Klaviermusikstil, der sich im Laufe der Zeit durchgesetzt hat und inzwischen auch von Musikern anderer Stilrichtungen anerkannt wird. Wer sich mit den folgenden Übungen beschäftigt, wird allerdings feststellen, daß nicht alle unter der Bezeichnung „Ragtime" veröffentlichten Musikstücke auch wirkliche Ragtimes sind.

Der echte Ragtime ist nicht gerade einfach zu spielen, eine Tatsache, mit der sich so mancher Pianist anfreunden mußte. Die Verwendung von Synkopen beispielsweise deutet darauf hin, daß wir es nicht mit leichter oder minderwertiger Musik zu tun haben, sondern mit Musik, die rhythmisch recht differenziert und anspruchsvoll ist. Seine Abneigung gegen den Ragtime durch spöttische Bemerkungen zum Ausdruck zu bringen, zeugt nicht gerade von einem hohen Maß an Feinsinn und musikalischem Verständnis.

Ziel dieser Ragtime-Schule ist es daher, dem Liebhaber dieses Musikstils das ungewohnte und gleichzeitig faszinierende Gefühl des „Joplin-Rags" zu vermitteln.

Übung Nr. 1

Für eine wirkungsvolle Vortragsweise des Ragtimes sind die rhythmisch exakte Wiedergabe der Notenwerte und die gewissenhafte Beachtung aller Phrasierungszeichen unerläßlich. Da manche Spieler in dieser Hinsicht etwas nachlässig sind, soll im folgenden jedes Detail ausführlich erklärt werden.

Bei dieser Übung ist die jeweils letzte Sechzehntelnote eines jeden Taktes zur ersten des folgenden Taktes durch einen Haltebogen übergebunden. Das bedeutet: aushalten bis zum Gesamtwert der Sechzehntelnoten! Das obere System dient nur zur Verdeutlichung der rhythmischen Struktur und soll nicht gespielt werden. Die punktierten Linien, die von den synkopierten Noten zu den Sechzehntelnoten des oberen Systems verlaufen, zeigen die genauen rhythmischen Werte an. Man spiele zunächst langsam, bis man den rhythmischen Schwung erfaßt hat. Ein Ragtime sollte niemals schnell gespielt werden:

Übung Nr. 2

Diese Übung ist etwas schwieriger, besonders für diejenigen, die es mit der linken Hand nicht so genau nehmen und dazu neigen, die Begleitung zu improvisieren. Der erste Ton der rechten Hand hat hier die Länge von 3 Sechzehntelnoten. Die zweite Note muß rhythmisch exakt folgen und wird durch einen Haltebogen zur folgenden übergebunden. Diese rhythmische Aufteilung wird in der gesamten Übung konstant beibehalten:

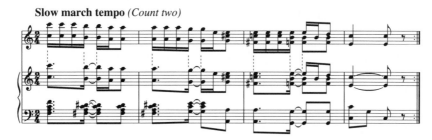

Übung Nr. 3

Die folgende Übung ist, wenn man sie sorgfältig ausführt, sehr effektiv. Um sie richtig wiedergeben zu können, sollte man sich zuerst über die genaue Zuordnung der punktierten Linien klar werden:

Übung Nr. 4

Hier wird durch die Überbindung der 4. und 5. Sechzehntelnote eines jeden Taktes eine Synkopierung erreicht. Der Synkopeneffekt ergibt sich natürlich nur, wenn der Bindebogen (Haltebogen) wie hier über Noten gleicher Tonhöhe steht. Im Gegensatz zu diesen Haltebögen bedeutet der Legatobogen lediglich enges Aneinanderbinden der Töne:

Übung Nr. 5

Der „Ragtime-Effekt" entsteht in diesem Beispiel durch den schweren Akzent auf der zweiten Note (Achtelnote) der rechten Hand und durch die Bindung der letzten Sechzehntelnote des Taktes an die erste des folgenden Taktes (über den Taktstrich hinweg). Dies ergibt einen schönen Effekt und ist keineswegs so kompliziert, wie es vielleicht auf den ersten Blick scheinen mag:

Übung Nr. 6

Die hier gegebenen Hinweise zur Ausführung des Ragtimes ermöglichen, in Verbindung mit den gestrichelten Linien, eine wirkungsvolle Interpretation der rhythmischen Vielfalt. Es kann nicht ausdrücklich genug darauf hingewiesen werden, daß der „Joplin-Ragtime" durch unachtsame oder fehlerhafte Ausführung zerstört wird. Selbst bei guten Spielern verliert er oft durch zu schnelle Ausführung völlig an Wirkung.
Alle diese Übungen wurden abgestimmt auf ein grundlegendes Ziel: daß jede Note so gespielt wird, wie sie geschrieben steht. Dieses und die sorgfältige Einhaltung der metrischen Unterteilungen ermöglichen erst eine sinnvolle und stilgerechte Ausführung:

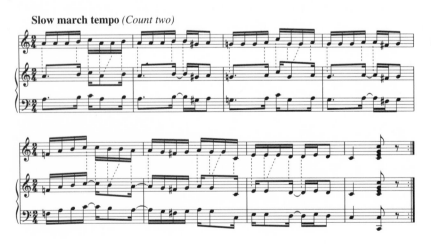

Méthode de Ragtime
de Scott Joplin

Remarque préliminaire

Ce que l'on a coutume d'appeler, d'un ton un peu dédaigneux parfois, le *Ragtime* est un style de musique pour piano qui s'est imposé au cours du temps, et qui est reconnu entre-temps par les musiciens des genres les plus divers. L'étude des exercices suivants montrera cependant que tous les morceaux caractérisés de *Ragtime* ne sont pas forcément vraiment des Ragtimes.
Le véritable Ragtime n'est pas simple à jouer, le pianiste devra s'en accommoder. L'utilisation de syncopes, par exemple, souligne le fait que nous n'avons pas affaire ici à une musique légère ou de valeur moindre. Se moquer du ragtime n'est pas vraiment le signe d'une sensibilité et d'une culture musicale élevées.
L'objectif de cette méthode est de transmettre à l'amateur de ce style de musique le sentiment inhabituel et fascinant à la fois du «Joplin Rags».

Exercice No 1

L'effet de l'interprétation des Ragtimes dépend entièrement de l'exactitude de la restitution rythmique de la valeur des notes et du respect consciencieux de tous les signes de phrasé. Certains interprètes étant un peu négligents à cet égard, chaque détail sera expliqué ci-après.
Dans cet exercice, la double croche de chaque mesure est reliée à la première note de la mesure suivante par l'intermédiaire d'une ligature. Cela signifie: tenir jusqu'à la valeur totale des deux doubles croches! Le système supérieur sert seulement à mettre en relief la structure rythmique et ne doit pas être joué. Les lignes en pointillés allant des notes syncopées aux doubles croches du système supérieur indiquent les valeurs rythmiques exactes. On jouera tout d'abord lentement, jusqu'à ce que l'on ait pris l'élan rythmique. Un Ragtime ne doit jamais être joué rapidement:

Exercice No 2

Cet exercice est un peu plus difficile, en particulier pour ceux qui ne prêtent pas suffisamment d'attention à la main gauche et tendent à improviser l'accompagnement. La première note de la main droite a ici la longueur de 3 doubles croches. La deuxième note doit suivre avec un rythme exact et elle est liée à la suivante par l'intermédiaire de la ligature. Cette répartition rythmique est conservée de manière constante pendant tout l'exercice:

Exercice No 3

Exécuté avec soin, l'exercice suivant fait beaucoup d'effet. Pour pouvoir le rendre correctement, prendre tout d'abord conscience de l'attribution exacte des lignes en pointillés:

Exercice No 4

Ici, on obtient une syncope grâce à la liaison de la 4ème et de la 5ème double croche de chaque mesure. L'effet de syncope n'apparaît, naturellement, que si la ligature est placée, comme c'est le cas ici, sur des notes de même hauteur. Au contraire de ces ligatures, le coulé signifie seulement une relation étroite des notes:

Exercice No 5

L'effet Ragtime est créé, dans cet exemple, par l'accent lourd sur la deuxième note (croche) de la main droite et par liaison de la dernière double croche de la mesure à la première de la mesure suivante (au-delà de la barre de mesure). Ceci donne un bel effet et n'est pas aussi compliqué qu'il peut y paraître à première vue:

Exercice No 6

Les indications données ici pour la réalisation du Ragtime permettent, en relation avec les lignes en pointillés, une interprétation pleine d'effet de la variété rythmique. On ne saurait souligner assez le fait que le «Joplin-Ragtime» est détruit par une interprétation inattentive ou fausse. Interprété trop rapidement, il perd souvent tout son effet, même chez de bons interprètes.

L'ensemble de ces exercices a été adapté en fonction d'un objectif fondamental: chaque note doit être jouée telle qu'elle est écrite. Seules cette condition et la répartition soigneuse des divisions métriques permettent une interprétation judicieuse et répondant aux critères du style:

1. The Entertainer

A Ragtime Two Step

Scott Joplin
1868–1917

Intro
Not fast

2. Elite Syncopations

Scott Joplin

3. Original Rags

Scott Joplin

4. Pine Apple Rag

Scott Joplin

5. The Cascades

Scott Joplin

6. Maple Leaf Rag

Scott Joplin

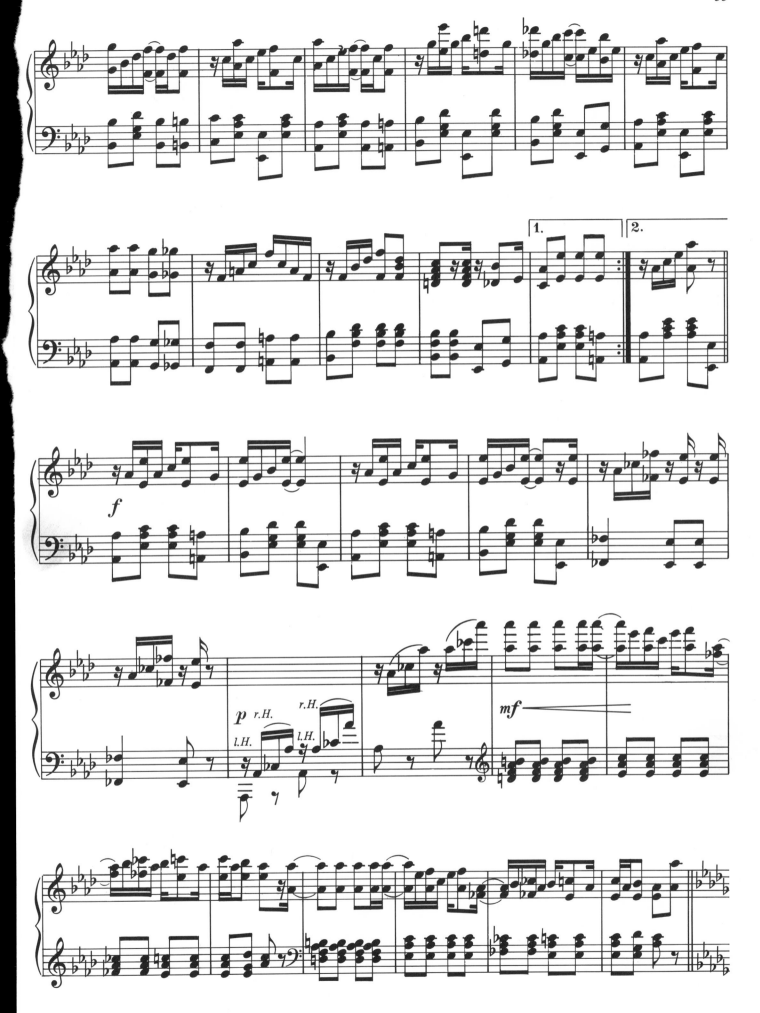

Trio